Which One

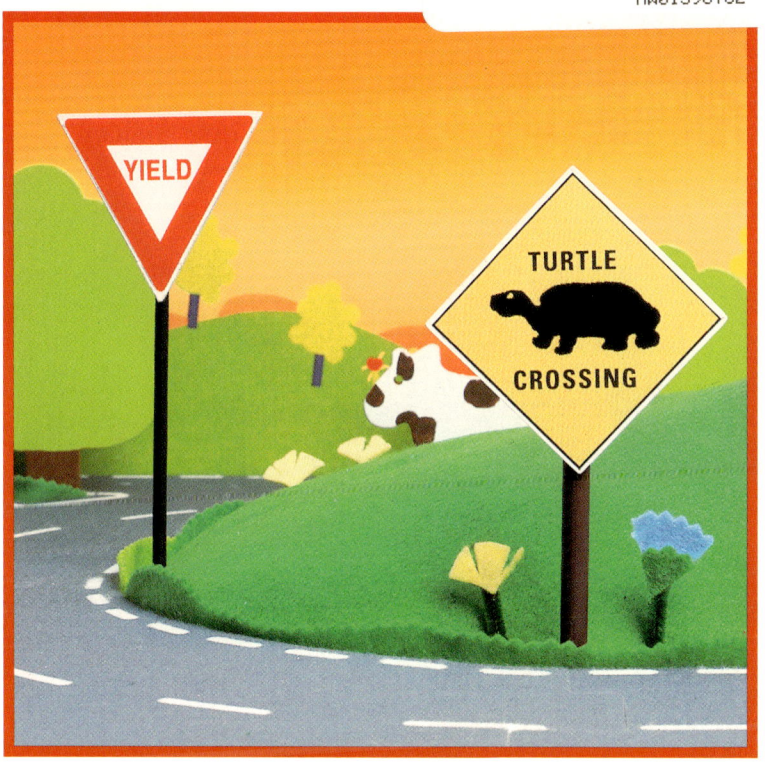

Linda Ekblad

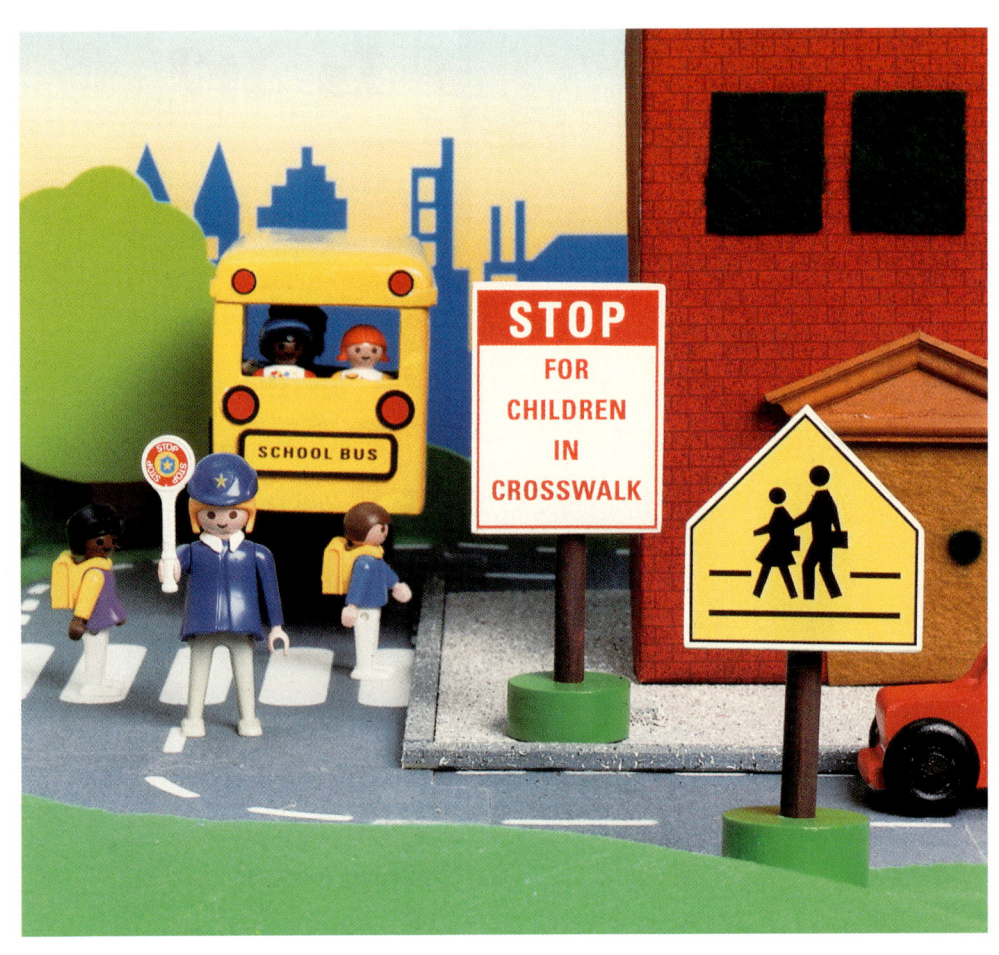

Which sign has five sides?

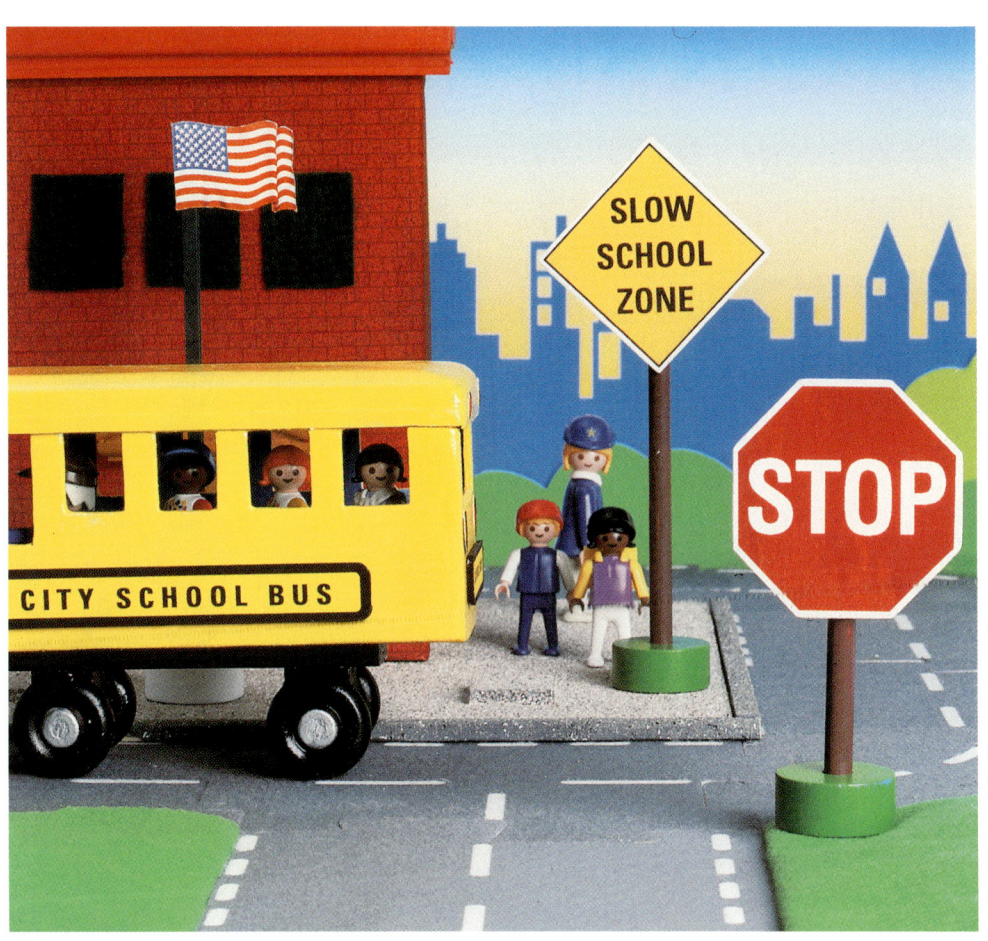

Which sign has eight sides?

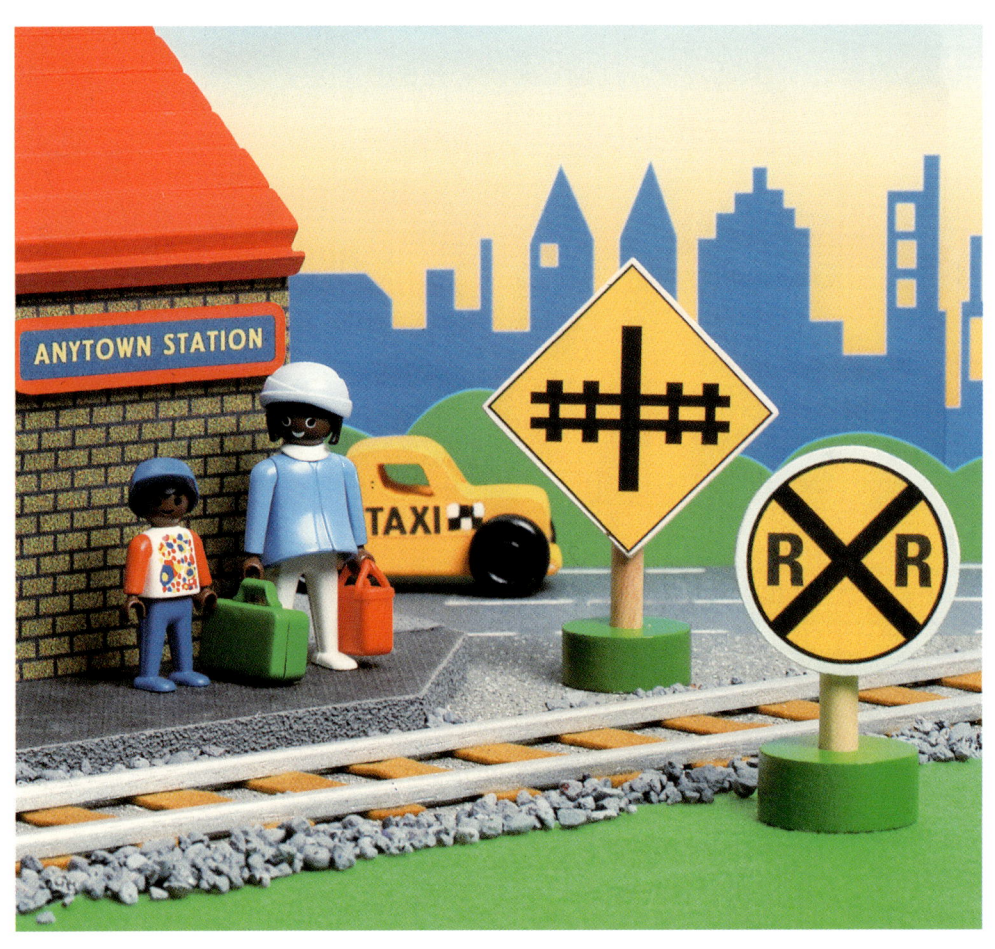

Which sign has four corners?

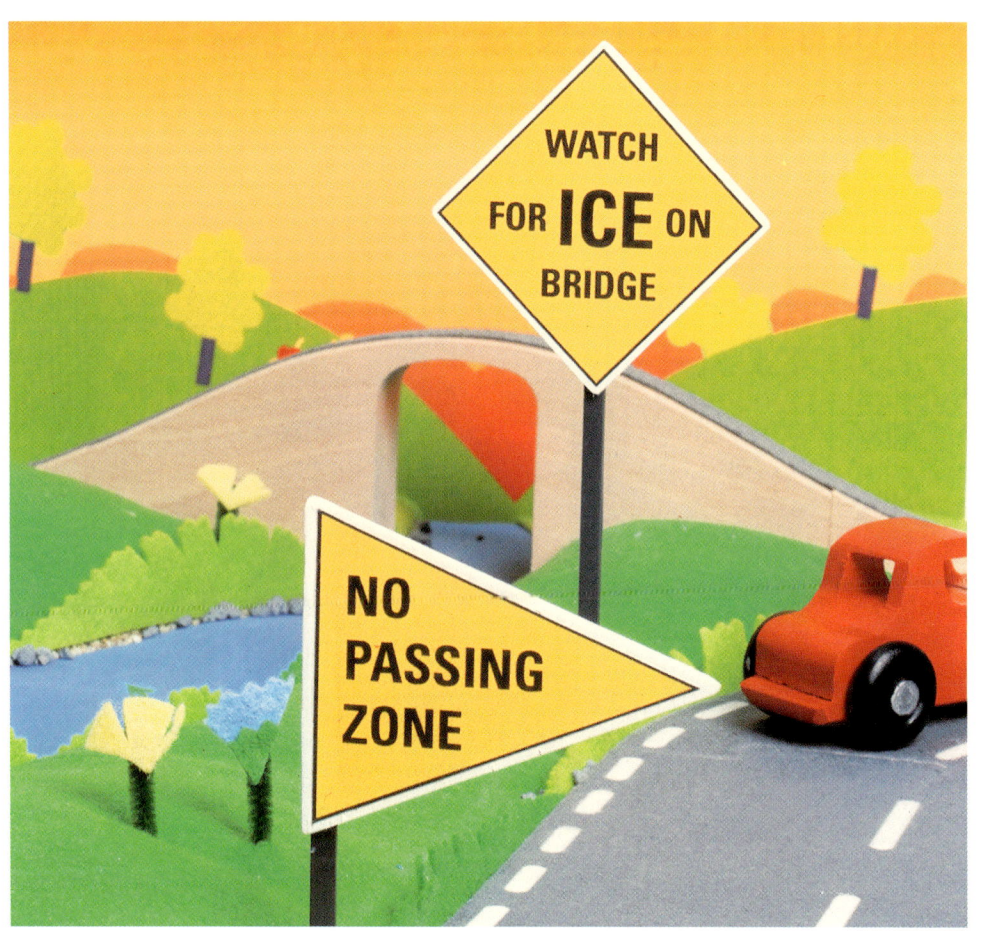

Which sign has three corners?

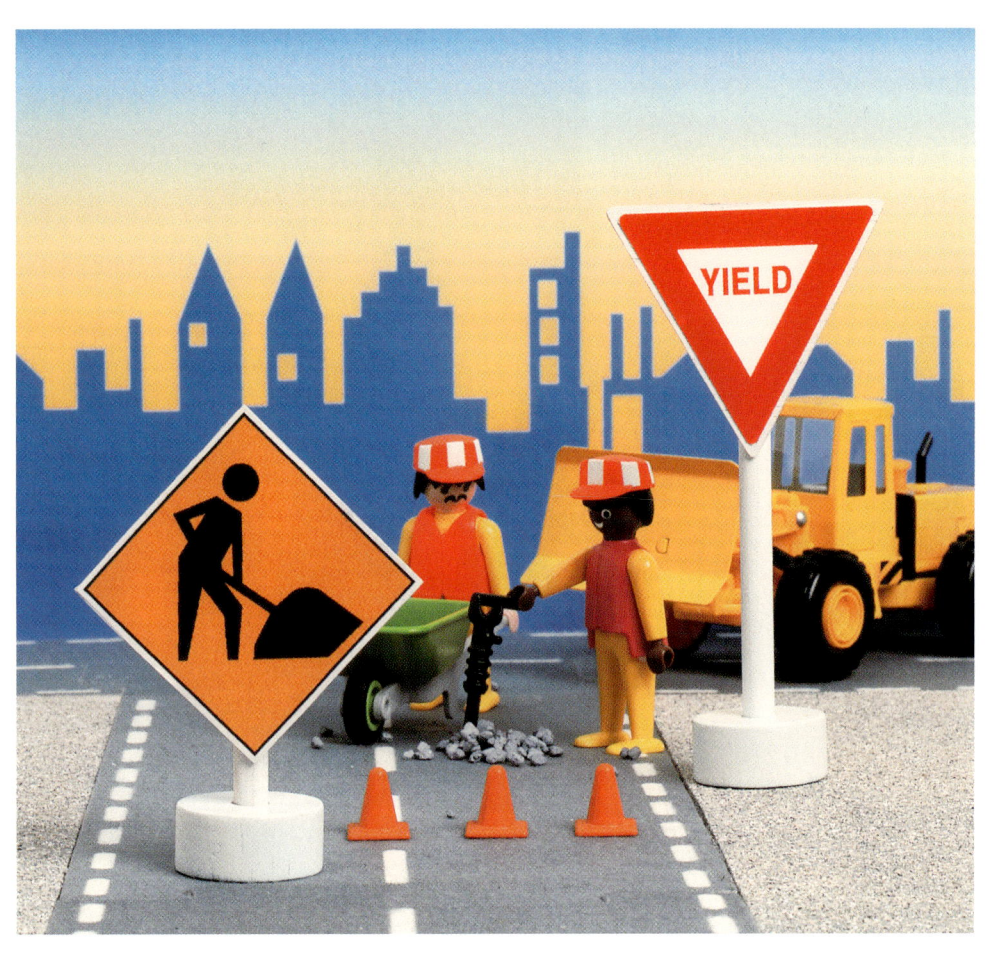

Which sign is a triangle?

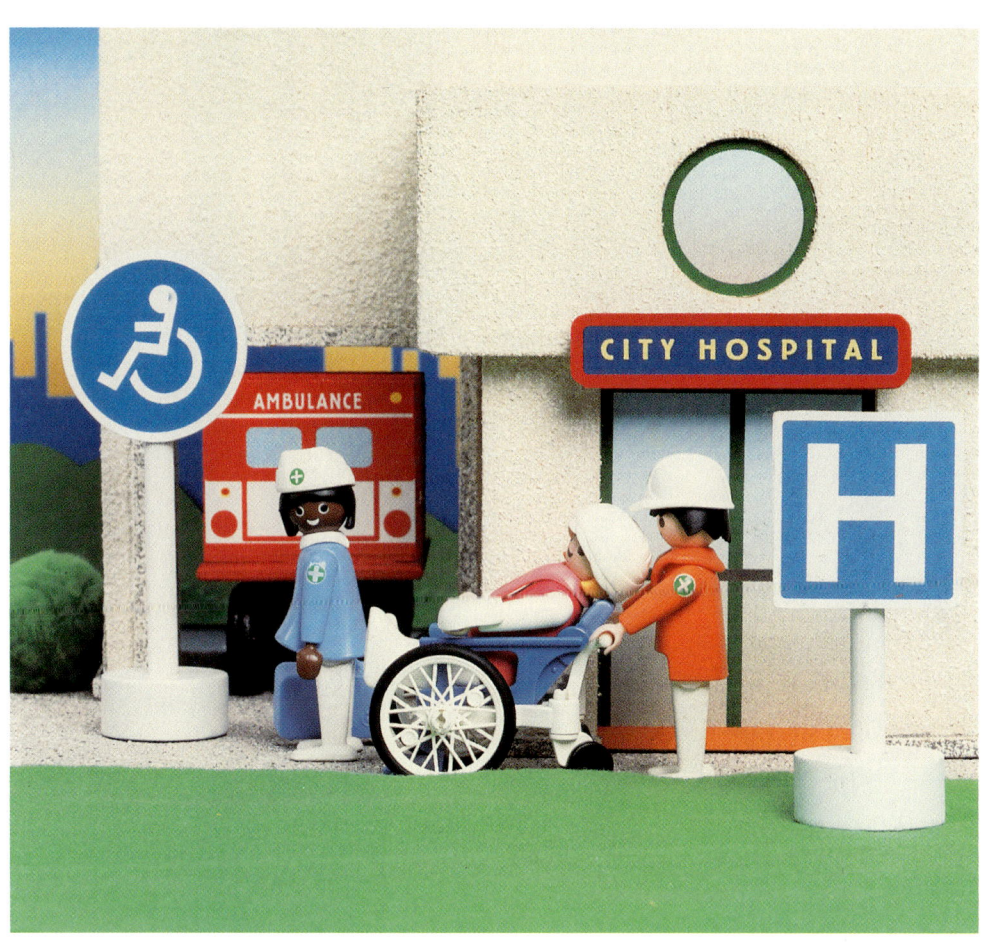

Which sign is a square?

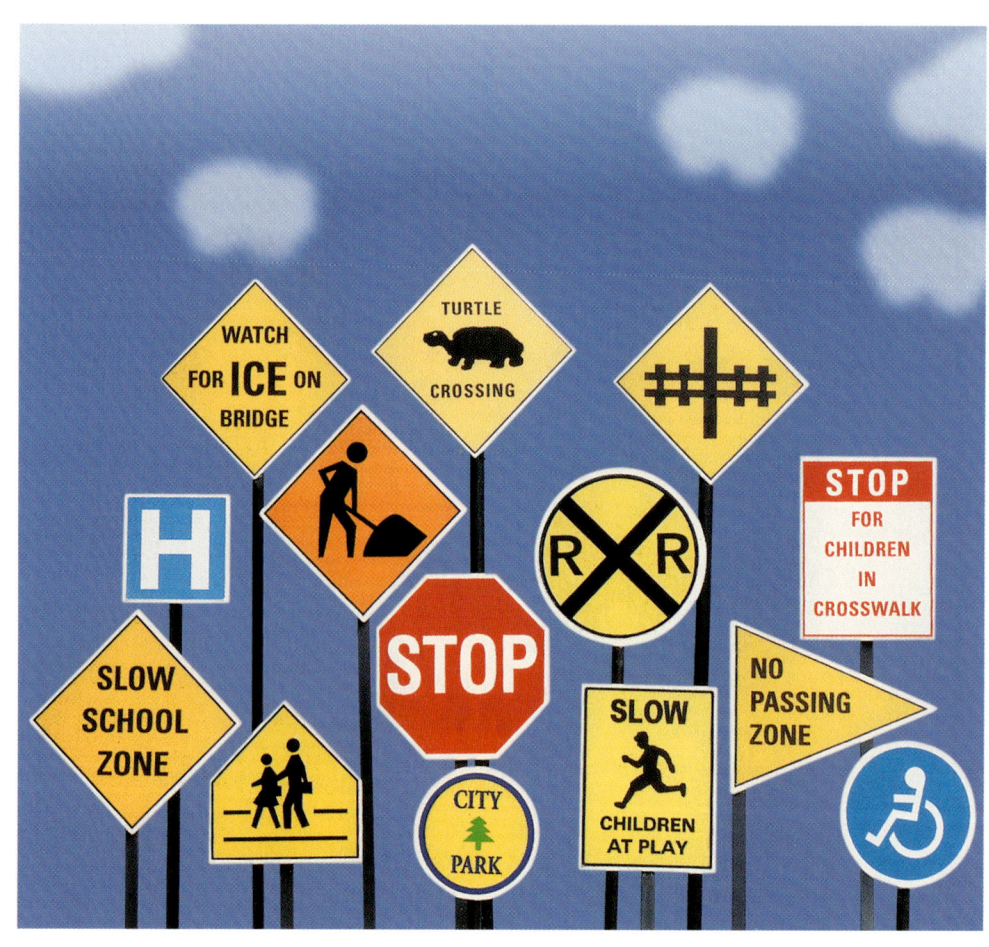

Signs have many shapes.